# Inside and Out

ROBERT B. RUDDELL

MARK TAYLOR

ELEANORE K. HARTSON

## ALLYN AND BACON, INC.

BOSTON   ROCKLEIGH, N.J.   ATLANTA   DALLAS   BELMONT, CALIF.

## Acknowledgments

Grateful acknowledgment is made to the publishers, authors, or copyright holders for permission to use and adapt the following materials in this book:

"Sing a Song of People," from *Songs of the City* by Lois Lenski. © copyright 1956 by Lois Lenski. Used by permission of Henry Z. Walck, Inc., publishers.

"George and Martha," adapted from *George and Martha* by James Marshall (text and illustrations). Copyright © 1972 by James Marshall. Reprinted by permission of the publisher Houghton Mifflin Company.

"The Toll Taker," copyright © 1963 by Patricia Hubbell. From *The Apple Vendor's Fair*. Used by permission of Atheneum Publishers.

"Mr. Pine's Mixed-Up Signs," adapted from *Mr. Pine's Mixed-Up Signs* by Leonard Kessler. Copyright © 1961 by Grosset & Dunlap, Inc. Used by permission of Grosset & Dunlap, Inc.

"Let's Ride the Bus," from *The Life I Live* by Lois Lenski. Copyright 1965 by Lois Lenski. Used by permission of Henry Z. Walck, Inc., publishers.

"Maybe I'll Be," © 1974 by Patty Zeitlin.

(continued on page 236)

Cover Design: Fujita Design, Inc.

Cover Illustration: Jackie Geyer

2 3 4 5 6 7 8   84 83 82 81 80 79 78

# Contents

**FEELING GOOD!**

Sing a Song of People (A Poem)   *Lois Lenski*                2

George and Martha   *James Marshall*                        6

Katy and Sam                                                13

   Where Is Sam?                            17

Judy Is Jody Is Judy                                        24

   Sometimes Different                      30

Mei Ling in the Middle                                      36

   A Kitten Helps                           40

   FRIENDS                                  46

   FEELINGS                                 48

**MAYBE I'LL BE**

The Toll Taker (A Poem)   *Patricia Hubbell*               50

The Bim-Bam Circus                                         52

Sarah Jack                                                 62

Mr. Pine's Mixed-Up Signs   *Leonard Kessler*              71

   Fix-Up the Mix-Up                        78

Let's Ride the Bus (A Poem)   *Lois Lenski*                82

The Day Nothing Much Happened                              86

Maybe I'll Be (A Song)   *Patty Zeitlin*                   94

   MAYBE I'LL BE                            96

   MIXED-UP SIGNS                           98

## ONCE THERE WAS AND WAS NOT

| | |
|---|---|
| The Coconut Game | 100 |
| The Three Billy Goats Gruff (A Play) | 107 |
| The Baby Beebee Bird   *Diane Massie* | 115 |
| Riddles (riddles)   *Rodney Peppe* | 124 |
| The Fat Cat   *Jack Kent* | 127 |
| THE STORYMAKING MACHINE | 140 |
| MONKEY HEAR, MONKEY DO | 142 |

## HERE AND THERE

| | |
|---|---|
| People | 144 |
| Simon Rodia | 149 |
| Castle in My City (A Song)   *Patty Zeitlin* | 157 |
| Alex the Painter | 160 |
| I Read It in a Book! | 172 |
| Who Are the People? (A Poem)   *Mark Taylor* | 182 |
| A BAD DAY | 186 |
| HOW TO WRITE A BOOK | 188 |

## WHERE THE WIND BLOWS

| | |
|---|---|
| Weather Is Full of the Nicest Sounds (A Poem)   *Aileen Fisher* | 190 |
| The Salad | 193 |
| Who Has Seen the Wind? (A Poem)   *Christina G. Rossetti* | 205 |
| Take a Look at Ants   *Gray Johnson Poole* | 206 |
| Ants Live Here (A Poem)   *Lilian Moore* | 216 |
| Quiet on Account of Dinosaur   *Jane Thayer* | 217 |
| THE BIG SALAD | 229 |
| FRIENDLY FACES, FRIENDLY PLACES | 230 |

Feeling Good !

# Sing a Song of People

Sing a song of people
Walking fast or slow;
People in the city,
Up and down they go.

People on the sidewalk,
People on the bus;
People passing, passing,
In back and front of us.
People on the subway
Underneath the ground;
People riding taxis
Round and round and round.

People with their hats on,
Going in the door;
People with umbrellas
When it rains and pours.

People in tall buildings
And in stores below;
Riding elevators
Up and down they go.

People walking singly,
People in a crowd;
People saying nothing,
People talking loud.
People laughing, smiling,
Grumpy people, too;
People who just hurry
And never look at you!

4

Sing a song of people
Who like to come and go;
Sing of city people
You see but never know!

—Lois Lenski

5

# George and Martha

*by James Marshall*

Martha liked to make pea soup.

Sometimes she made it all day.

Pots and pots of pea soup.

If there was one thing

    George did not like,

    it was pea soup.

George hated pea soup

    more than anything in the world.

But it was so hard to tell Martha.

7

One day George had to eat

    Martha's soup.

He ate and ate soup.

Then he said to himself,

    "I can not stand any more pea soup.

    Not one more drop."

8

Martha was in the kitchen.

So George put the rest of his soup

into his shoes under the table.

"Now she will think I ate it,"

he said to himself.

But Martha saw him from the kitchen.

"How can you go home
with pea soup in your shoes?"
Martha said.
"Oh, my," said George.
"You saw me."
"You did not tell me
that you hate my pea soup,"
said Martha.
"I did not want you to feel bad,"
said George.

10

"Don't be silly," said Martha.

"Good friends can always tell

each other

how they feel and what they think.

I will tell you something, George.

I hate pea soup, too.

But I do like to make it.

From now on

you will not have to eat it."

"Oh, I'm so glad!" said George.

"Would you like some cookies?"
  said Martha.
"Oh, that would be great!"
  said George.
"Then you will have them,"
  said his friend.

# Katy and Sam

Katy lived in a house by the sea.

She lived with Father and Mrs. Day.

Mrs. Day took care of things for them.

Father worked very hard.

Lots of times he had to be away.

Most of the time Katy was alone.
When Father was at home,
he liked to play with her.
They would take walks on the sand
and go sailing.
But when Father was away,
Katy had to do things by herself.
There was no one to play with.

14

One summer day,

    Katy met a sea gull.

Katy talked to the sea gull.

The next day

    Katy met the sea gull again.

They got to be good friends.

Katy called him Sam.

Katy and Sam talked every day.

Now Katy did not feel all alone.

She had a friend to play with.

She had a friend to talk to.

She had Sam.

Now she was happy.

## Where Is Sam?

"I have a friend,"

    Katy said one day.

"Who is your friend?" said Father.

"He is Sam," said Katy.

    "He is a sea gull."

"I'd like to meet him," said Father.

"Maybe you can," said Katy.

    "I'll have to ask him."

One fall day, Father had to go away.

"I can meet Sam when I come back,"
   he told Katy.

Then Sam went away, too.

Katy called him and looked for him.

She looked for him every day.

But Sam did not come.

That made Katy feel very bad.

18

Katy could not forget Sam.

What did Sam do in the rain?

Where did Sam sleep at night?

Where did Sam go in the day?

When Father came back, he said,

"Can I meet Sam now?"

"No," said Katy sadly.

"Sam went away."

Winter came.

Katy looked for Sam every day.

She missed him very much.

"I hope Sam will come back,"
    said Katy.

"I don't think Sam will come,"
    said Mrs. Day.

"Yes, he will," said Katy,
    "because he's my friend."

One spring day, Father said,

    "Let's go sailing."

Katy liked to sail.

Katy and Father sailed all day.

They saw many sea gulls.

One of the gulls came to Katy.

It was Sam!

Katy was glad to see him.

"How do you know this is Sam?"
said Father.

"I just know," said Katy.

Sam went home with them.

He did not go away.

Sam made a nest in the garden.

"He wants to be with me," said Katy.

The next day, Sam had a surprise
    for Katy.
There were three eggs in the nest!
"Sam is a lady sea gull," said Father.
    "You could call her Samantha."
"No," said Katy.
    "She is still Sam.
    She will always be Sam to me."

# Judy Is Jody Is Judy

Judy and Jody were twins.

No one at school could tell

who was who.

"Am I talking to Judy or Jody?"

the teacher would ask.

"Are we playing with Judy or Jody?"

friends would ask.

One day Aunt Dee and Aunt Bee
came to stay for a few days.
Aunt Dee and Aunt Bee
were twins, too.
They always did everything the same.

"It's nice that Judy and Jody
   are twins just like us,"
   said Aunt Dee and Aunt Bee.
   "When they grow up,
   they will do everything the same.
   Just like us!"

26

Judy looked at Jody.

Jody looked at Judy.

"Oh, no!"

Judy and Jody said at the same time.

That night they had a talk.

"I like you, Jody," said Judy.

"I like you, too," said Jody.

"But sometimes I just want to be me,"
    said Judy.

"That's just how I feel, too,"
    said Jody.

"Let's be different," said Judy.

"Yes, let's," said Jody.

28

So Judy and Jody were different

    right away.

Judy went to sleep

    with her head at the top of the bed.

Jody went to sleep

    with her head at the bottom.

At last they were not just the same!

## Sometimes Different

Judy and Jody were twins,

    but they wanted to be different

    from each other.

One morning Judy did look different.

Jody looked different, too.

When Judy talked,

    she talked very low and very slow.

When Jody talked,

    she talked very high and very fast.

Aunt Dee and Aunt Bee were surprised.

They were twins,

and they were always the same.

"Twins should be just like each other,"

said Aunt Dee and Aunt Bee.

"Well, I'm me," said Judy.

"And I'm me," said Jody.

At school, Judy jumped rope
    and learned to stand on her head.
Jody painted a big picture
    and learned how to make
    silly animals.

That night, they showed
Aunt Dee and Aunt Bee
the things they had learned.
"Twins should learn the same things,"
said Aunt Dee and Aunt Bee.
"Twins should do the same things."
"Not always," said Judy.
"Today I did something different
that I can teach Jody."
Then Jody said,
"I learned something different
that I can show Judy."

33

"It's good to be different," said Judy.

"We can do more things that way,"
    said Jody.

"Maybe that is so,"
    said Aunt Dee to herself.

"That is something to think about,"
    said Aunt Bee to herself.

The next morning, what a surprise!

Aunt Dee looked different.

She looked just like herself.

Aunt Bee looked different, too.

She looked just like herself.

That was a nice surprise.

# Mei Ling in the Middle

Everything was new to Mei Ling.

She lived in a new apartment.

She went to a new school.

And she had two new friends.

Pam lived upstairs.

Nancy lived downstairs.

And Mei Ling lived in the middle.

Pam and Nancy
      did not like each other.

They would not talk to each other.

"Nancy is silly," Pam would say.

"All she likes to do is read."

And Nancy would say,

"Pam is dumb.

All she likes to do is play ball."

"Well, I like to play ball,"

said Mei Ling.

"And I like to read books."

Mei Ling told her mother
about her two friends
who hated each other.
"What will I do?" she said.
"Do your best," said Mother.

So Mei Ling did her best.

One day she would play with Pam.

One day she would play with Nancy.

"It's the best I can do,"

     she told her mother.

     "I'm right in the middle.

     I live in the middle apartment.

     And I am in the middle

     of two people who hate each other.

     I am Mei Ling in the middle."

And so she was!

# A Kitten Helps

One morning on the way to school,
  Mei Ling and Pam saw a kitten
  on top of a big bin.
When the kitten saw them,
  it began to run and jump.
All at once the kitten fell into the bin!
The bin was very deep.
The kitten began to cry.

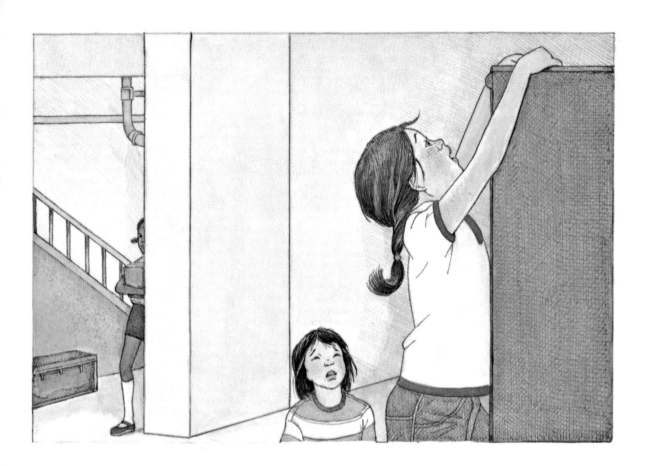

Pam said,

    "I'll get that box over there.

    Hold it for me, Mei Ling,

    while I try to reach the kitten."

Pam got on the box.

"I can see the kitten," she said,

    "but I don't think I can reach it."

All at once, Pam fell into the bin!

"Help!" called Pam.

Just then Nancy came by.

Mei Ling told her about the kitten
and Pam.

"I'll help," Nancy said.

Nancy got on the box
and reached into the bin.

"Give me the kitten,"

she said to Pam.

Nancy took the kitten from Pam.

Then she helped Pam

get out of the bin.

"Thanks," said Pam.

"That's all right," said Nancy.

They all laughed.

"You talked to each other,"
said Mei Ling.
"Let's all be friends together.
O.K. ?"

Mei Ling was happy.
Now they were all friends.
Pam was the upstairs friend.
Nancy was the downstairs friend.
And Mei Ling was still the friend
in the middle.

# Friends
## Rhyming Time

Friends care
and _____.

Friends live to _____.

Friends are here, there
and _____.

46

Friends find
    ways to be _____.

Friends go walking
    and _____.

Here's the thing,
    friends are _____.

| | |
|---|---|
| share | talking |
| everywhere | everything |
| give | kind |

47

# Feelings

How would you feel?
Tell your friend or teacher.

You find a dime.
A boy hits you.
Mother hugs you.
Someone says you are bad.
Dad smiles at you.
You fall off your bike.

bad
sad

happy
glad

mad
upset

48

# Maybe I'll Be

# The Toll Taker

Roll down your window,

Hand the man a dime,

We're coming to the tollbooth

And we're next in line.

Will the man say "thank you"?

Will the man smile?

Won't he even look at us

Just for a while?

Child, he's busy counting,
Child, he's making change.
But can't he even look at us?
Life is very strange.

—Patricia Hubbell

# The Bim-Bam Circus

Mr. Bim was the head
   of the Bim-Bam Circus.
Mr. Bim was not happy.
"Why are you not happy?"
   asked Mrs. Bim.
"No one comes to the circus,"
   said Mr. Bim.
   "That is why I am not happy."

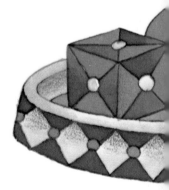

"Hello, Mr. Bim," said a tall lady.

"I am Terry Blue.

I have a TV show.

I want you to be on my show

with some of your animals."

Mr. Bim was very happy.

"When should we come?"

he asked Miss Blue.

"Tomorrow at three," she said.

Mr. Bim told the circus people
the good news.
"People will see us on TV,"
he said.
"Then they will come to the circus."
This made the circus people
very happy.

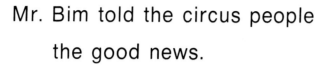

The next day they went
    to the TV studio.
Mr. Bim drove the circus truck
    with all the people
    and animals inside.
He had to go very slow.

55

All at once the truck stopped.

Mr. Bim could not make it go.

"Oh, no!" said Mr. Bim.

　　"We will be late for the show!"

56

The elephant man said,
  "Emma the elephant
  can pull the truck."
People smiled when they saw
  Emma pulling the truck.
They all began to follow her.

57

Miss Blue was at the studio.

"You are late, Mr. Bim,"
   she said.

"Yes, I am," said Mr. Bim.
   "My truck would not go."

"That is too bad," said Miss Blue.

"It is too late to do my show

in the studio."

The snake lady said,

"You could do your show

at the circus."

"Let's do that!" said Miss Blue.

"Let's have my show at the circus!"

That night Mr. Bim and Mrs. Bim
talked with Miss Blue on TV.
"You have a great circus,"
said Miss Blue.
"We think so, too," said Mr. Bim.
"It isn't the biggest circus."
"But it's the best!"
said Miss Blue.

Many people saw the TV show.

They were glad to know

　about the Bim-Bam Circus.

So every night people came to see it.

Mr. Bim was very happy.

He had a new sign made that said:

　THE BIM-BAM CIRCUS.

　NOT THE BIGGEST BUT THE BEST!

# Sarah Jack

Sarah Jack liked to climb trees.

That is why she had a job

    picking apples for Mrs. Terry.

Mrs. Terry had two apple trees

    in her garden.

And they had lots of apples on them.


Sarah Jack saw a boy by the wall.

He was Horrible Hank.

The kids called him Horrible Hank

    because he was a big pest.

"Look who's in the tree!" called Hank.

"Go away!" said Sarah Jack.

"O.K., but give me some apples,"
   said Hank.

"No," said Sarah Jack.

   "I'm picking them for Mrs. Terry."

All at once Horrible Hank
   climbed over the wall.
He took the ladder away from the tree
   where Sarah Jack was picking.
He put the ladder by the other tree
   and climbed up.
Horrible Hank began to take
   Mrs. Terry's apples.

"Get out of that tree," said Sarah Jack.

"They are not your apples."

"So what?" said Horrible Hank.

"You'll see!" said Sarah Jack.

With that, Sarah Jack climbed
out of the tree.

She took the ladder away from the tree
where Horrible Hank was picking.

Then she went to the back door
and let out Mrs. Terry's dog.

Little Tip wasn't very big,
but he made a lot of noise.

He jumped up and down under the tree.

Horrible Hank was afraid to climb down.

Sarah Jack told Mrs. Terry
    about Horrible Hank.
Together they made a plan.
"Sarah Jack tells me you have come
    to help pick apples," she said.
"I did?" said Hank.
"Just fill the bag with apples
    and give it to Sarah Jack,"
    said Mrs. Terry.
Hank picked and picked.

68

At last, Mrs. Terry said,

"You can stop now.

Do you want to pick apples tomorrow?"

"No!" said Horrible Hank.

Sarah Jack put the ladder by the tree.

Horrible Hank climbed out of the tree

and went home.

Mrs. Terry and Sarah Jack
had a good laugh.
"I don't think Horrible Hank
will want to take apples any more,"
laughed Mrs. Terry.
Tip growled, as if to say,
"Not if I'm around!"

# Mr. Pine's Mixed-Up Signs

*by Leonard Kessler*

Mr. Pine made signs.

He made signs that said Stop.

He made signs that said Go.

He made signs that said Fast.

He made signs that said Slow.

Mr. Pine made all the signs
   in Little Town.

71

He made signs for streets
and signs for stores.
He made big signs and little signs.
He made signs with words
and signs with pictures.
Little Town had all the signs
a town could need.

But the signs got old.

They were hard to read.

"We need new signs,"

   said the Mayor of Little Town.

So he went to see Mr. Pine.

"Mr. Pine," said the Mayor,

    "will you make new signs

    for Little Town?"

"Yes, I will," said Mr. Pine.

    "I like to make signs.

    I will make them all.

    I will put them up, too."

74

Mr. Pine worked very hard.

He made many new signs

for Little Town.

When it was time to put up the signs,

Mr. Pine could not find his glasses.

"Where are my glasses?" he said.

He looked here and there

and everywhere.

But he could not find them.

75

"Where can they be?" he said.

"My, my, everything looks so funny!

I wish I had my glasses."

Everything did look funny.

But Mr. Pine had to put up the signs.

So out he went.

76

Soon the new signs were up
　　all over Little Town.
How funny they looked!
Mr. Pine did not know it,
　　but the signs were all mixed up!

# Fix-Up the Mix-Up

"What can this be?" said a man.

"Look at that!" said a lady.

"Look at the signs!"

said all the people of Little Town.

"They are all mixed up!"

"Find Mr. Pine!" cried the Mayor.

"Find him fast!"

78

Mr. Pine was looking for his glasses.

He looked and looked.

"Did I put them here?

  Or did I put them there?" he said.

  "I must find them.

  I want to see my fine new signs."

Mr. Pine even looked in the dog house.

The dog had his glasses!

Mr. Pine put on his glasses.

He went to look at his new signs.

"Oh, no!" he said.

   "They are all mixed up!"

"Mr. Pine," said the Mayor,

   "look at your signs."

"I will fix them right away,"

   said Mr. Pine.

Mr. Pine went to work.

Soon the new signs

    were in the right places.

Soon Little Town looked all right.

But no one will forget

    Mr. Pine's mixed-up signs.

# Let's Ride the Bus

Bus stop at the corner,
Just stand right there and wait;
Here it comes, door opens,
Hop in and don't be late.

Hop in, hop out!
Hear the driver shout.
There's room for more
Don't block the door.
Hop in, hop out!

Have your money ready,
Just drop it in the slot;
Find a seat that's empty,
Or stand up like as not.

Bus starts up. It's going!
It can't go very fast.
All the trucks and autos
And taxis going past.

83

Now it's going faster,
You'd better hang on tight;
Going round the corner,
Hold on with all your might.

Now it's going slower,
It's coming to your stop;
Time to ring the buzzer,
Get up and out you hop.

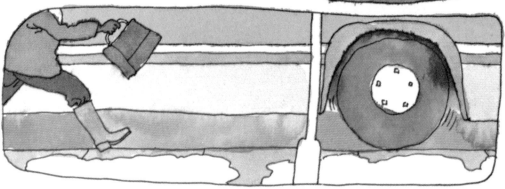

Hop in, hop out!

Hear the driver shout!

There's room for more,

Don't block the door.

Hop in, hop out!

—*Lois Lenski*

# The Day
# Nothing Much Happened

"Nothing has happened today,"

   said Susan.

"But today isn't over," said Mr. Miles.

   "Maybe something will happen yet."

Susan and Dad were

   in the Miles' garage.

Susan looked at the big tow truck.

On it was painted:

   THE FRIENDLY MILES.

Sometimes Susan helped Dad.

It was fun to ride in the truck.

Sometimes she and Dad helped people
with cars that were stuck.

Sometimes they had to fix flat tires.

Susan was always a big help to Dad.

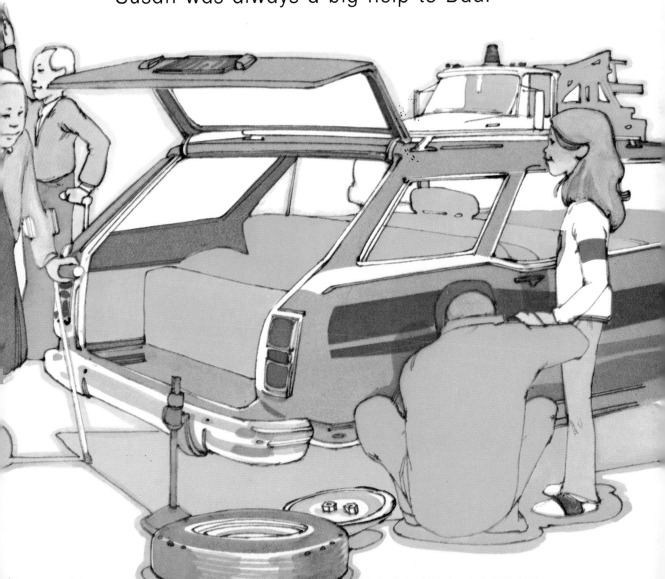

Mr. Miles got a call.

"Hello," said Mr. Miles.

"A plane is on the freeway?
We'll come right away."

Mr. Miles smiled at Susan and said,

"Let's go!"

There was a plane right in the middle
of the freeway!

Cars could not go around it.

The police were there.

But the police car was stuck.

Susan helped Dad with the police car,
and she helped him with the plane.

When the plane took off,
all the people were glad.

They all said,

"Thanks to the Friendly Miles
everything is fine!"

When Susan and Dad got back
to the garage, there was a call.
"Your car will not go?" said Dad.
"We will be right there."
"Let's go, Susan," said Dad.
"A lady needs our help."
It was raining very hard,
and now it was dark.

When they came to a house,

  Susan said, "This is our house, Dad!"

"Yes, it is," said Dad,

  "and there is the lady with the car

  that will not go."

The lady was Susan's mother!

"I'm glad to see you!" said Mother.

"Thanks to the Friendly Miles,

everything will be fine!"

"That's right," said Susan.

"We help everyone.

Mothers, too."

"What happened today?" asked Mother.

"Not much," said Susan.

"Just a stuck police car."

"Just a plane on the freeway,"
said Dad.

"Just a lady with a car
that would not go," said Susan.

"As you can see," said Dad,
"nothing much happened."

"Oh, that's too bad," said Mother.

And the Friendly Miles laughed
and laughed.

93

# Maybe I'll Be

(FOR GUITAR, CAPO I FINGERING IN E)

May - be I'll be a sing - er,___ and play a pret - ty gui - tar.___

May - be I'll be an as - tro - naut, ride a rock - et to a star.

May - be I'll be a pain - ter, paint a mur - al___ on the wall. And

may - be I'll be the en - gi - neer___ on the Wa - bash Can - non Ball.

94

Maybe I'll be an author,
and write a good long book.
Maybe I'll run a restaurant,
or be a gourmet cook.
Maybe I'll be a dancer
in a famous concert hall.
Maybe I'll be the engineer
on the Wabash Cannon Ball.

Maybe I'll be a plumber,
and fix the sinks that leak.
Maybe I'll be a carpenter,
and build a house a week.
Maybe I'll be a fireman—
hear my siren call.
Maybe I'll be the engineer
on the Wabash Cannon Ball.

Maybe I'll be a doctor,
a dentist, or a nurse.
Maybe I'll be a poet
with a pocket full of verse.
A teacher, or a tailor,
or none of those at all.
Maybe I'll be the engineer
on the Wabash Cannon Ball.

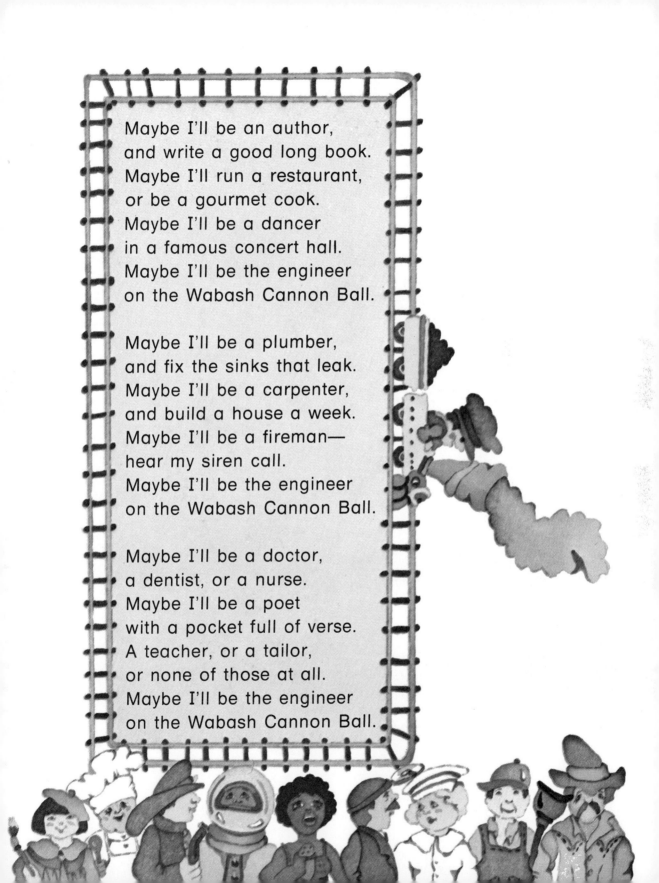

# Maybe I'll Be. . . .

Think about it. Act it out.
Let your friends guess what you will be.

## working with people

actor          mayor          athlete

## working with people and things

dentist          salesperson          officeworker

## working with things

chemist 96          trucker          carpenter

mother       park ranger       teacher

firefighter       farmer       baker

inventor       astronomer       artist

97

# Mixed-up Signs!

Can you fix them?
Write the signs on your paper.
Put in *a,e,i,o,* or *u* where they fit.
Now read what they say.

FINE FOODS

Fresh m__lk and f__sh
to put on your d__sh.

We sell l__gs,
l__cks, m__ps
but no s__cks.

HARDWARE

SMITH'S

We have r__gs
but no b__gs.

PET STORE

Food for f__t
c__ts and r__ts.

5&10¢ STORE

P__ns are
t__n c__nts.

98

# Once There Was
# and
# Was Not

# The Coconut Game

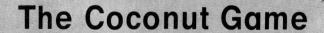

One day Elephant fell into a pit.

"Help!" cried Elephant.

The animals ran and looked
   into the pit.

"We can't help you, Elephant,"
   they said.

      "You are too big.

      And the pit is too deep."

The animals could not help Elephant.

One by one they went away.

"Elephant!" called Monkey
from the top of the pit.
"I'll get you out."
"But how?" asked Elephant.
"You are so little."
"Not too little," said Monkey.
And away she ran.

Soon Monkey came back.

She had a ladder with her.

Elephant tried to climb up the ladder.

But when he got on it,
    the ladder broke.

"It's no use," said Elephant.
    "How will I get out of this pit?"

"You will see," said Monkey.

And away she ran.

Soon Monkey came back.

She had a rope with her.

Elephant took hold of the rope.

Then Monkey pulled on it.

But Monkey could not

    pull Elephant out of the pit.

"It's no use," said Elephant.

    "How will I get out of this pit?"

"You will see," said Monkey.

And away she ran.

Soon Monkey came back.

Many, many monkeys were with her.

Each monkey had a coconut.

"Let's play the Coconut Game,"
    said Monkey.

Monkey began to roll a coconut
    into the pit.

All the other monkeys began
    to roll coconuts into the pit.

"Why are you rolling coconuts
    into this pit?" cried Elephant.

Elephant was very angry.

He stomped on the coconuts.

He jumped up and down
    on the coconuts.

Elephant grew more and more upset.

But still the monkeys rolled coconuts
    into the pit.

105

All at once Elephant found himself
close to the top of the pit.
He walked right out of it!
All the monkeys laughed and jumped.
"Didn't you know that someone small
can help someone big?"
asked Monkey.
"No," said Elephant.
"But now I do!"

# The Three Billy Goats Gruff

## A Play

Players:  Reader

First Billy Goat Gruff

Second Billy Goat Gruff

Third Billy Goat Gruff

Troll

Stage Hand

Time:  Morning

Place:  In the country

You will need:

1. Three *signs*

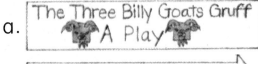
a. The Three Billy Goats Gruff — A Play

b. To The Hills

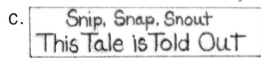
c. Snip, Snap, Snout This Tale is Told Out

2. A *bridge* made of three chairs
   or two chairs and a board

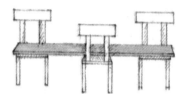

3. A *tripping sound* made from two
   wood blocks or any noise maker

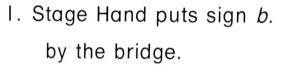

Getting ready:

1. Stage Hand puts sign *b.*
   by the bridge.

2. Reader sits on the floor and
   opens book.

3. Troll gets under the bridge.

4. The three Billy Goats get ready
   on left side of bridge.

5. Listeners are seated.

6. All is quiet.

The words in a box

   tell you something to *do.*

All the other words tell you

   something to *say.*

The play begins:

| Stage Hand holds up sign *a.* |
|---|

**Reader:** Once there were three Billy
   Goats Gruff who wanted to go
   to the hills beyond
   to make themselves fat.

**First Billy Goat:** This morning
   I am going to the hills beyond.
   That is where the grass is green
   and thick.
   I will eat until I'm fat.

**Reader:** But the billy goat had
to cross over a bridge.
A mean old troll lived under it.

First Billy Goat walks across the
bridge with fast steps.

Stage Hand makes tripping sound:
trip, trip, trip, trip.

**Reader:** Trip-trap, trip-trap
went the bridge.

**Troll:** Who's that tripping
over my bridge?

**First Billy Goat:** It's only the tiniest
Billy Goat Gruff.
I'm going to the hills beyond
to make myself fat.

**Troll:**  Now I'm coming to gobble
   you up!

**First Billy Goat:**  Don't eat me.
   I'm too little, that I am.
   Wait for the second Billy Goat Gruff.
   He's much bigger.

**Troll:**  Very well. Be off with you!

Second Billy Goat walks across the
bridge with plain steps.

Stage Hand makes tripping sound:
trip, trap, trip, trap, trip, trap.

**Reader:**  Trip-trap, trip-trap went
   the bridge.

**Troll:**  Who's that tripping over
   my bridge?

**Second Billy Goat Gruff:** Oh, it's I, the second Billy Goat Gruff. I'm going to the hills beyond to make myself fat.

**Troll:** Now I'm coming to gobble you up!

**Second Billy Goat:** Don't eat me! Wait until the big Billy Goat Gruff comes. He's much bigger.

**Troll:** Very well. Be off with you!

Third Billy Goat walks across the bridge with slow and loud steps.

Stage Hand makes tripping sound: TRIP-TRAP, TRIP-TRAP, TRIP-TRAP.

**Reader:** TRIP-TRAP! TRIP-TRAP!
went the bridge.

**Troll:** Who's that tripping
over my bridge?

**Third Billy Goat:** It's I! The big
Billy Goat Gruff!

**Troll:** Now I'm coming
to gobble you up!

**Third Billy Goat:** Well, come on!
I'm not afraid of you.
I'll punch you with my feet
and toss you with my horns!

Troll and Billy Goat fight.

**Reader:** The Third Billy Goat Gruff
threw the troll into the river.

Troll falls down. Third Billy Goat goes on his way and joins the other two.

**Reader:** And that was the end of the troll.

The three Billy Goats Gruff ate and ate until they grew very fat.

The Three Billy Goats join hands and dance in a circle.

Stage Hand holds up sign *c*.

**Reader:** Snip Snap Snout, This Tale is Told Out!

P. S.
We hope you liked the show!

# The Baby Beebee

*by Diane Massie*

The animals at the zoo had roared
and growled all day long.
They were very tired.
"It's time to go to sleep,"
said the      .
Soon the zoo was very still.

115

"Bee bee bobbi bobbi!

Bee bee bobbi bobbi!"

"What," said the , "is that?"

"It's the baby beebee ,"

said the .

"He's new to the zoo."

"Well, tell him to be quiet,"

growled the .

"I want to sleep."

"Bee bee bobbi bobbi!

Bee bee bobbi bobbi!"

"Be quiet, please," said the .

"But I can't,"

said the baby beebee .

116

"I'm wide awake.

Bee bee bobbi bobbi,

bee bee bobbi bobbi."

"Quiet!" roared the  .

"He's wide awake," said the  .

"Why isn't he tired like the rest

of us?" growled the  .

"Aren't you tired?"

asked the  .

"No," said the baby beebee  ,

"I was sleeping all day long.

Now it's time for me to sing.

Bee bee bobbi bobbi,

bee bee bobbi bobbi!"

117

"Oh, dear," said the  ,
   "I am so tired."
"Bee bee bobbi bobbi,
   bee bee bobbi bobbi,"
   went the baby beebee .
"Quiet!" yelled all the animals.
   "We can't sleep!"
"Bee bee bobbi bobbi,
   bee bee bobbi bobbi,"
   went the baby beebee
   all night long.

In the morning the animals
were very tired.
"What has happened?"
said the keeper.
"The  is still asleep.
The  is standing on his head.
The  won't play.
Dear me!"
"Bee bee bobbi bobbi,"
said the baby beebee
one more time.
Then he went to sleep.

119

The animals talked quietly
to each other.
They looked at the baby beebee  .
He was sleeping.
"Bee bee bobbi!" roared the  .
"Bee bee bobbi!" called the  .
"Bee bee bobbi!" growled the  .
"Bee bee bobbi bobbi!"
yelled all the animals together.
"Quiet," said the baby beebee 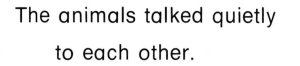 .

"I am trying to sleep."

"Bee bee bobbi bobbi!"

yelled the animals.

The keeper ran up.

"What is it now?" he said.

But no one could tell him.

All day long the animals yelled,

"Bee bee bobbi bobbi."

The baby beebee

could not sleep at all.

The  went down and
the ☾ came up.
"Bee bee bobbi bobbi," said the 🦁
very quietly.
He was too tired to roar.
"Bee bee bobbi bobbi,"
said the 🐟 very quietly.
He was too tired to talk.
"Beebee," said the 🐹 .
He was too tired to say more.
And then all was still.

The  looked down
on a sleeping zoo.
Not a ~~~ moved.
Not an ~~~ moved.
Not a ~~~ moved.
And the baby beebee ~~~
was asleep high up in his tree.
Night is best for sleeping,
even for very little beebee ~~~ .

123

# Riddles

Round as a biscuit, busy as a bee,

You can guess every riddle,

But you can't guess me.

[A Clock]

What has a mouth,

But cannot eat?

[A Doll]

124

What has a face,
But cannot see?

[A Clock]

What has legs,
But cannot walk?

[A Chair]

125

Round as an apple,
Flat as a chip,
Got two eyes,
And can't see a bit.

[A Button]

What loves a dog and rides
    on his back;
He can travel for miles and not leave
    a track?

[A Flea]

—Rodney Peppe

126

# The Fat Cat

*by Jack Kent*

One day an old woman
    was cooking some soup.

She had to go next door.

"Would you look after the soup?"
    she asked the cat.

"I'll be glad to," said the cat.

The old woman went next door.

The soup looked so good
    that the cat ate all of it.

And the pot, too!

When the old woman came back,
she said to the cat,
"Where is the soup?"
And the cat said,
"I ate the soup and the pot, too.
And now I'll eat you!"
And he ate the old woman.

Then he went for a walk.

On the way he met Skohottentot.

Skohottentot said to him,

"What have you been eating,

my little cat?

You are so fat."

The cat said, "I ate the soup,

    and the pot,

    and the old woman, too.

    Now I'll eat you!"

So he ate Skohottentot.

Next he met Skolinkenlot.

Skolinkenlot said to him,

"What have you been eating,

my little cat?

You are so fat."

"I ate the soup, and the pot,
   and the old woman, too,
   and Skohottentot,"
said the cat.
   "Now I'll eat you!"
So he ate Skolinkenlot.

Next he met five birds together.

"What have you been eating,

my little cat?

You are so fat."

"I ate the soup, and the pot,

   and the old woman, too,

   and Skohottentot, and Skolinkenlot.

   Now I'll eat you."

And he ate the five birds together.


Next he met seven girls dancing.

"Little cat," they said,

   "you are so fat.

   What have you been eating?"

"I ate the soup, and the pot,

   and the old woman, too,

   and Skohottentot, and Skolinkenlot,

   and five birds together.

   Now I'll eat you."

And he ate the seven girls dancing.

Next he met a lady
     with a pink parasol.
"Little cat," she said,
     "you are so fat.
     What have you been eating?"
"I ate the soup, and the pot,
     and the old woman, too,
     and Skohottentot, and Skolinkenlot,
     and five birds together,
     and seven girls dancing.
     Now I'll eat you."

And he ate the lady
with the pink parasol.

Next he met a man.

"Little cat," said the man,

"you are so fat.

What have you been eating?"

"I ate the soup, and the pot,

and the old woman, too,

and Skohottentot, and Skolinkenlot,

and five birds together,

and seven girls dancing,

and the lady with the pink parasol.

Now I'll eat you."

"No," said the man.

"You will not eat me."

Then the man cut open the cat.

Out jumped the lady with the pink
    parasol,

    and the seven girls dancing,

    and the five birds together,

    and Skolinkenlot, and

    Skohottentot.

And the old woman took her pot,

    and her soup,

    and went home.

# The Storymaking Machine

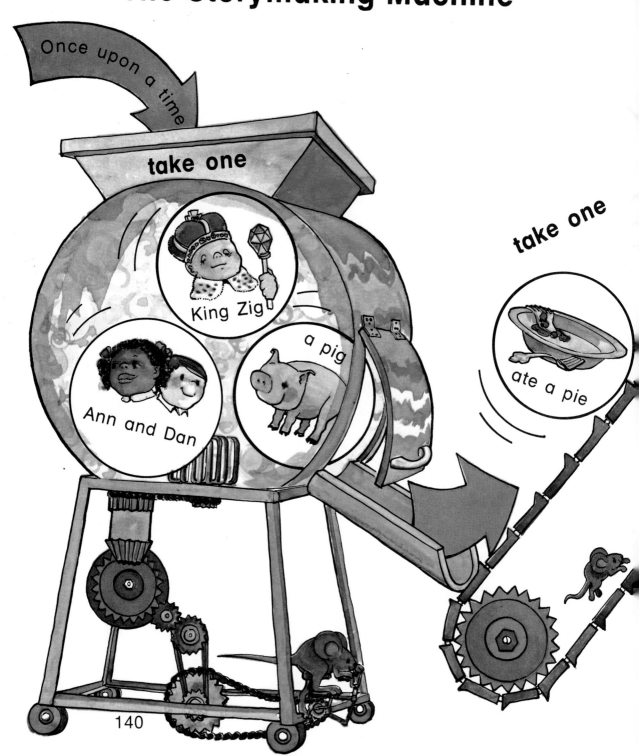

Once upon a time

take one

King Zig

Ann and Dan

a pig

take one

ate a pie

140

# Monkey Hear, Monkey Do

Play the monkey game.

It goes like this:

Say: "Monkey is big."
What does your voice do?
Yes, your voice goes down.
When your voice goes down,
    Monkey sits down.

Say: "Is Monkey big?"
What does your voice do?
Yes, your voice goes up.
When your voice goes up,
    Monkey's tail goes up.

Now say these sentences.
Tell what Monkey will do.

Cat is fat              Elephant will eat
Is cat fat              Will elephant eat

142

# Here and There

# People

There are all kinds of people
everywhere.
Each of them is somebody.
People can be fathers,
and mothers,
and children.

People can be neighbors.

And people can be friends.

Everywhere there are friends.

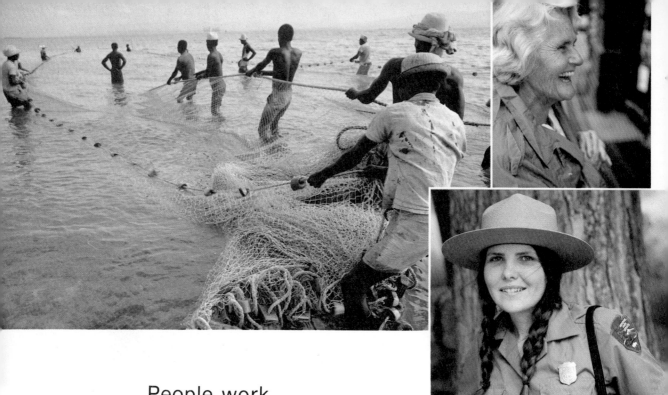

People work,

and people play.

People are different in many ways.

And people are the same in many ways.

146

People live in different kinds
   of houses,
   and in different places.
Everywhere there are people,
   sometimes the same,
   sometimes different.

Everyone is somebody.

You are somebody, too.

Who?

148

# Simon Rodia

Near the middle of Los Angeles
  are some beautiful towers.
The towers were made
  by a man named Simon Rodia.
This is his story.

Simon worked hard all his life.

He worked to make
    houses and buildings beautiful.

After work he liked to read.

He would read about people
    who made beautiful things.

150

Simon saw all the kinds of junk
people did not want.
He began to take the junk home.
He took old bottles, plates,
cups, and spoons.
He took bottle caps, nails,
wire, and old pipe.
He began to build with the junk.

Simon worked very hard.

By the time he was an old man,

   he had made the beautiful towers.

They looked like the towers

   of a wonderful castle.

One day Simon moved away.

The people who lived near the towers

saw him no more.

But every time they looked

at the towers,

they would think of him.

Children came to play

    in the towers.

Some people did not want them to.

They said the towers were not safe.

They said the towers

    should be pulled down.

But other people said, "No!"

One day a big truck came
to pull down the beautiful towers.
The truck pulled and pulled.
The towers did not move.
The truck pulled and pulled.
The towers did not fall down,
but the truck broke!
The people laughed and were glad.

155

Simon's towers still stand
like wonderful castles.
They are called the Watts Towers.
People from all over the world
come to look at them.
Simon Rodia was a good man.
He made something beautiful
for everyone.
People will not forget him.

# Castle in My City

*Joyfully*

There's a cas-tle in my ci-ty____ there's a cas-tle in my town, so strong and so pret-ty____ they can't tear it down; it looks to me like can-dy and turn-ing car-ou-sels; its tow-ers are san-dy and cov-ered with shells.

Mr. Simon Rodia,

A poor man and old,

Built all its towers

Without any gold.

Funny scraps like bottle caps

Gave him great pleasure;

Shiny glass and water taps

And things children treasure.

The castle is for children—

For me and for you.

The castle is for anyone

Who makes it come true.

A funny fence or circus tents,

Kingly crowns or cages;

It's bound to be

What you want to see,

No matter what your age is.

(Repeat beginning of first verse)

159

# Alex the Painter

Alex didn't know what to do.

Everybody was doing something.

His father was at work.

His mother and his sister, Rosa,
    were talking with friends.

His brother, Alberto,
    was building a boat.

160

Alex wanted to help with the boat.

"Not now, Alex," said Alberto.

"Next week you can help me paint it."

"I'll look for some paint,"

Alex said to himself.

When he found some cans of paint,

he had an idea.

161

He took the cans of paint

and walked to the park.

In the park were some buildings.

They were not very pretty.

"I will try a little painting,"

said Alex.

"Then I will know how to help Alberto

paint his boat."

162

Alex had a good time painting.
He made faces.
He made animals.
And he painted his name
over and over:
ALEX LAZARO

"What are you doing?"
asked a policeman.
"Painting," said Alex.
"What is your name, and where
do you live?" asked the policeman.

164

"Alex has been painting buildings
    in the park," said the policeman.

Alex's mother was upset.

So were Rosa and Alberto.

Alex did not feel too good.

Everybody looked at him.

When Alex's father heard about Alex,

he was upset.

"That was not right, Alex," he said.

"They were just old buildings,"

said Alex.

"But they don't belong to us,"

said his father.

"You must not do such a thing again."

166

"Alex needs something that is
fun to do," said Alberto.
"But he is too little to help me."
"I have an idea," said Rosa.
"Maybe Alex will like it."
"What is it?" asked Alex.
"Wait until tomorrow," said Rosa.
"It will be a surprise."

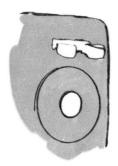

The next morning,
Rosa called someone.
Then she talked with Father.
"Yes, that is a good idea,"
said Father.
"I think Alex would like it."
Then Rosa said, "Come with me, Alex."
Away they went on the bus.

"This is Tony," Rosa told Alex.

"He is my good friend."

"Rosa tells me you like to paint,"
said Tony.

"Would you like to help me
paint pictures on buildings?"

"Yes!" said Alex.

169

"People pay me to paint pictures
on their buildings," said Tony.
"I will pay you to help me."
So Alex had a job helping Tony!
Tony and his helpers
painted every day.
Every day Alex helped them.

Then one day they began to paint
the buildings in the park.
They made the buildings look beautiful.
And Tony let Alex sign his name!

People came to look at the paintings.

They saw Alex's name on them.

Father was very happy for Alex.

"Well, you are a fine painter,"
    he said.

    "I will call you Alex the Painter."

"That's who I am," said Alex.

And Father gave him a great big hug.

# I Read It in a Book!

Once there was a little town
    on the side of a mountain.
Near the little town was a mine.
The men of the little town
    worked in the mine.
They worked very hard
    deep, deep down in the mine.

The little town looked sad.

There were hardly any trees.

There were no flowers.

And all the buildings were old.

The library was very old.

It was gray and dark,

    and nobody ever went there.

One day, on the way to school,

    a boy named Rap had a surprise.

He saw a fine new sign that said:

    FREE LIBRARY.

    COME ONE! COME ALL!

A lady was standing at the door.

She had a big smile.

"Hello," said the lady.

"I'm Ms. Plunkett, and I love books.

Do you like to read?"

"Not much," said Rap.

"I don't think books are much good."

"Maybe you will," said Ms. Plunkett.

"I'm going to make this library

a place to know and love."

When Rap came home from school,

Ms. Plunkett was painting the library.

"Where did you learn to paint

and make signs?" asked Rap.

"From books," said Ms. Plunkett.

"I learn lots of things from books."

"I don't," said Rap.

"Maybe you will," said Ms. Plunkett.

In a few days,

    things began to happen.

The children helped Ms. Plunkett

    paint the library and plant flowers.

And Ms. Plunkett told them

    many wonderful stories.

"How did you learn so many stories?"

    asked Rap.

"I read them in books," she said.

Soon everybody came for books.
Ms. Plunkett helped them find books
    that told how to fix cars,
    train dogs,
    make ice cream, give plays,
    build boats, and make a park.
So the people of the little town
    began to fix up everything.
Now things began to happen!

They painted their houses.

They planted trees.

They planted flowers everywhere.

If somebody learned something new,

   he would say, "I read it in a book."

The town looked better and better.

People did more and more things.

And they all looked

   more and more happy.

One day Rap told
Ms. Plunkett a secret.
There was something he wanted
to learn to do.
Ms. Plunkett found a book
that told how.
Rap read the book over and over.
He did what it said over and over.
Ms. Plunkett knew.
But she would not tell a secret.

One day the people
had a party for Ms. Plunkett.
The children gave a play.
Then Rap did magic tricks.
Learning magic was his secret.
"Where did you learn?" people asked.
"Where?" laughed Rap.
"I read it in a book!"

181

# Who Are the People?

Who are the people in cars?

I don't know.

How fast they go!

182

Along a freeway,

Down a street.

We never meet.

We just stare

And pass each other by.

I wonder, do they care

That I am I?

Who are the people in cars?

183

AND
Who are the people on stars?
I can't say.
They're far away!

184

Far in the sky,

Too far to walk,

Too far to talk.

We just stare

From here to there.

I wonder do they know

How much I care

Who the people are – on stars?

—Mark Taylor

# A Bad Day

Read the story.

Bill was late for his school bus. This was
　　the start of a bad day.
At school his best friend did not want to
　　play with him.
When Bill got home, he could not find his
　　pet rat. Mother helped him find the pet
　　rat.
Bill said, "Some days are like that."

Tell in what order things happened.

His best friend did not play with him.
Bill was late for the school bus.
Mother helped find the pet rat.
He could not find his pet rat.

- Think about a bad day you had.


- On your paper write a story about it.


- Read your story to a friend.

# How to Write a Book!

Write a book about a person.

Get:
- pencil or tape recorder
- crayons
- paper
- a person

Talk to your person

- Write or tell the story.
- Draw pictures.
- Make a cover for it.

# Where
# the Wind
# Blows

# Weather Is Full
# of the Nicest Sounds

Weather is full

of the nicest sounds:

it sings

and rustles

and pings

and pounds

and hums

and tinkles

and strums

and twangs

190

and whishes
and sprinkles
and splishes
and bangs
and mumbles
and grumbles
and rumbles
and flashes
and CRASHES.

I wonder
if thunder
frightens a bee,
a mouse in her house,
a bird in a tree,
a bear
or a hare
or a fish in the sea?

*Not me!*

—*Aileen Fisher*

192

# The Salad

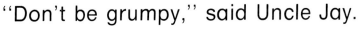

"This is hard work," said Max.

"It is hard to dig."

"It is hard to rake, too,"
said Carla.

"Don't be grumpy," said Uncle Jay.

"Making a good vegetable garden
is always hard work."

193

Uncle Jay was helping them

   plant a garden.

They were going to grow 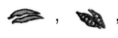 ,

 ,  ,  ,  ,

 , and 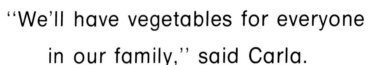 .

"We'll have vegetables for everyone

   in our family," said Carla.

"It will be a good garden," said Max.


They worked hard all day.

Uncle Jay showed them

   how to plant the seeds.

"You must water and weed this garden

   every day," he said.

   "You must take good care of it."

195

When the garden began to grow,
everybody in the family said,
"What a good garden it will be.
Fresh vegetables will be nice."

So Max and Carla worked hard
to water and weed the garden.
They wanted it to be the best garden
in the world.

But bad things began to happen.

Some days the sun was too hot.

Once Max gave the garden

  too much water.

Then bugs and pests began to eat

  the  plants.

The birds began to eat things, too.

It was all bad for the garden.

Max and Carla looked for bugs.

They tried to make the birds go away.

They did the best they could.

But the garden began to look very bad.

It made them pretty sad.

But Uncle Jay said, "Don't give up."

So they worked still harder.

Then one day some dogs
 ran all over the garden!
Max was so mad he began to cry.
They did their best to fix things.
But the garden was a big mess.

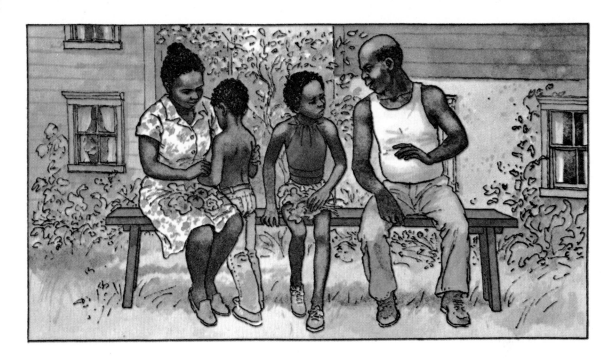

"We still have some  ,"

said Carla.

"And some  and some  ."

"We have a little bit of everything,"

said Max.

Uncle Jay said, "You did your best."

Mama said the family could always get

fresh vegetables at the store.

But it made Carla and Max

feel horrible.

One Sunday morning, Mama said,

"Everybody in the family is coming

for Sunday dinner."

Then Carla had an idea.

She told Max and Uncle Jay about it.

They said it was a good idea.

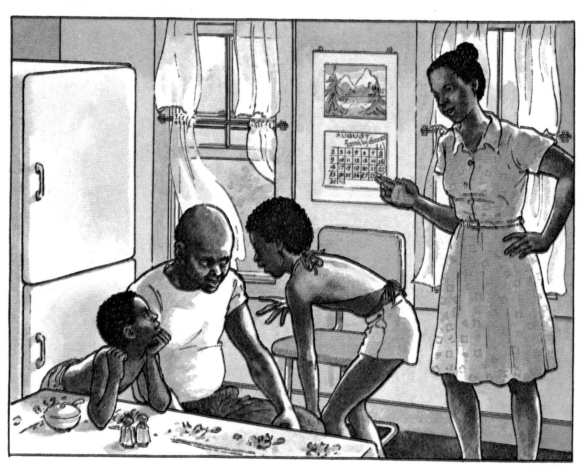

When everybody sat down to eat,

there was a great big salad of

 ,  , 🍅 , 🧅 ,

 , 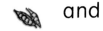 and  !

"What a wonderful salad!" they all said.

"Where did it come from

to look so fresh and good?"

"We grew it," said Carla.

"We had a bad time with our garden,"
    said Max, "but we did grow
    this big salad."

Everybody laughed.

"It's the best salad in the world!"
    they all said.

And it was so good,
    they ate it all up!

# Who Has Seen the Wind?

Who has seen the wind?
Neither I nor you:
But when the leaves hang trembling,
The wind is passing through.

Who has seen the wind?
Neither you nor I:
But when the trees bow down
their heads
The wind is passing by.

—Christina G. Rossetti

205

# Take a Look at Ants

by *Gray Johnson Poole*

Take a good look at ants.

Ants are everywhere.

There are many kinds of ants.

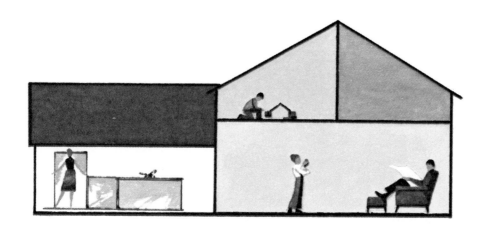

## Ants Make Nests

Ants are like people.

They do not live alone.

All ants make nests.

They live and work together

in a nest.

207

# Different Kinds of Nests

The pictures show three

different kinds of nests.

Some ants make holes in trees

for nests.

Some ants make nests
from leaves.

Many ants dig nests
in the ground.

# Life in the Nest

Each ant in the nest has a job.

The mother is the queen.

Her job is to lay eggs.

The eggs grow into workers.

The workers take care of the queen.

They feed her and clean her.

They dig holes and make new rooms.

Some ants take care of the eggs.

Other ants take care of the nest

and keep it safe.

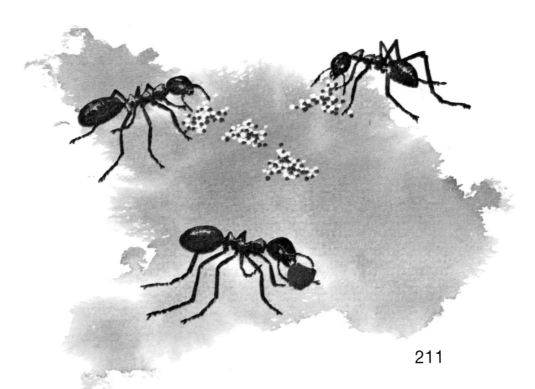

# Life Out of the Nest

Workers leave the nest.

They look for food.

Some ants eat big bugs.

They chew the bugs into parts.

Then they take the parts

back to the nest.

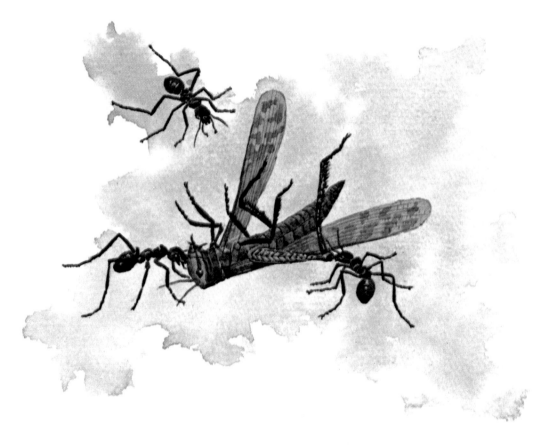

Some ants take parts of leaves
and flowers to the nest.
Others take back juices
from flowers.
And some ants take seeds
back to the nest.
An ant can pick up food
much larger than itself.
Ants are very strong.

## Ants Talk to Each Other

Ants are like people in another way.

They talk to each other.

They rub parts of their bodies
together.

They make a high noise
that other ants can hear.

People can sometimes
hear these sounds, too.

# Things for You to Do

1. Look for ants.

2. See where they go.

3. See how they get food.

4. Try to find where they live.

# Ants Live Here

Ants live here
by the curb stone,
see?
They worry a lot
about giants like
me.

—Lilian Moore

216

# Quiet on Account
# of Dinosaur

*by Jane Thayer*

What Mary Ann liked best in school
was reading about dinosaurs.
"If I could just find a dinosaur,"
she said.
One day she saw a cave.
She saw something sticking out
of the cave.
Mary Ann pulled on it and
out came a big dinosaur.

Mary Ann wanted to take
the dinosaur home.
She had him follow her.
A plane flew overhead.
It made a big noise,
and the dinosaur was afraid.
But Mary Ann told him
all about planes.

218

A big truck roared by them.

The dinosaur jumped.

He was afraid of the truck.

But Mary Ann told him about trucks.

Next a train went by.

The dinosaur was so afraid

    he wanted to run away.

"That's just a train," said Mary Ann.

Soon the dinosaur was all right.

They came to Mary Ann's house.

"May I keep him for a pet?"
   asked Mary Ann.

"No!" said Mother.

"Then I'll take him to school,"
   said Mary Ann.

220

The next day Mary Ann
    took the dinosaur to school.
She went in to tell the class.
"Where is he?" everyone cried.
"He's outside," said Mary Ann.

When it was time for lunch,
the children ran outside.
"What is his name?"
asked the children.
Mary Ann looked at the dinosaur
and said,
"His name is Dandy.
May we keep him for a pet, Ms. Tutt?"
"Why, yes," said Ms. Tutt.

Soon there was a story about Dandy
    in the town paper.
People from miles around
    came in cars and trucks
    and planes and vans
    to see Dandy.
Now there was a lot of noise.
Cars went roaring by.
People were yelling.
Dandy no longer seemed happy.
He would hide his head and shake
    when people came to see him.

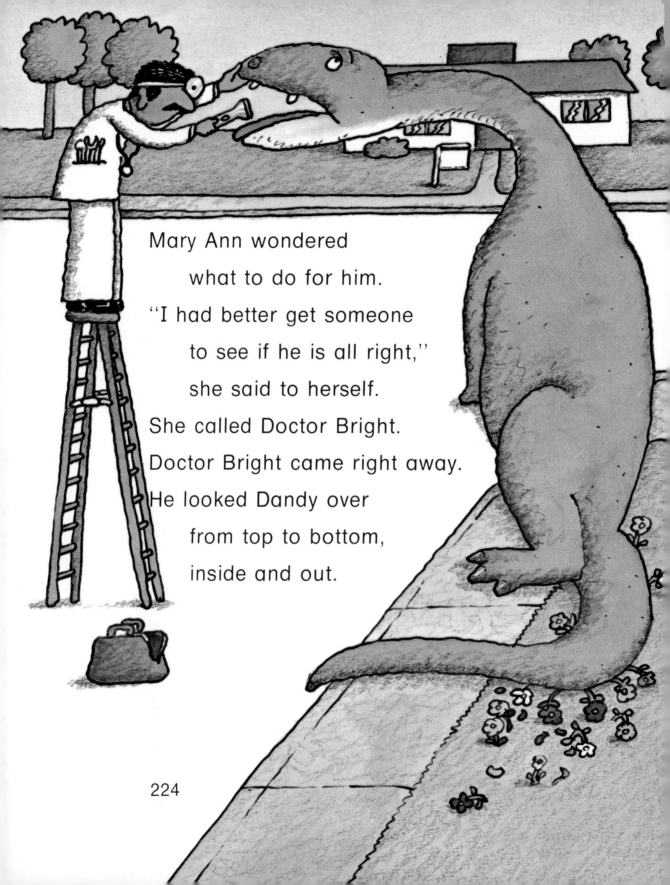

Mary Ann wondered
what to do for him.
"I had better get someone
to see if he is all right,"
she said to herself.
She called Doctor Bright.
Doctor Bright came right away.
He looked Dandy over
from top to bottom,
inside and out.

224

Just then a car roared by
 filled with people to see Dandy.
Dandy began to run away.
"He may be afraid of people,"
 said Doctor Bright.
 "I'll look after him for a few days."
Doctor Bright and Mary Ann
 put Dandy in the school gym.

When Dandy got to the gym,

    he stopped shaking.

"He feels better!" cried Mary Ann.

    "I think I know why!"

"It was the noise," said Doctor Bright.

    "Dandy is afraid of noise."

"You're right," said Mary Ann.

    "Dandy is afraid of things

    that make noise,

    like cars and trucks

    and trains and planes.

    In the days of dinosaurs there were

    no loud noises like that!"

Mary Ann had the children

    help her make a big sign

    that said:

    QUIET ON ACCOUNT OF DINOSAUR.

That made Dandy very happy.

227

Mary Ann was happy, too.
Having a dinosaur was better
than reading about a dinosaur.
And Mary Ann made up her mind
to be a dinosaur scientist
when she grew up.
And she was!

# The Big Salad

What's in the big salad?
The story can be told with a picture graph.

| | | | | | |
|---|---|---|---|---|---|
| onions | | | | | |
| lettuce | | | | | |
| peppers | | | | | |
| tomatoes | | | | | |
| spinach | | | | | |

How much lettuce is in the salad?
How many tomatoes were cut?
What other vegetables were used?

What's in the salad dressing?
Make a picture graph of it.

salt

pepper

229

oil          vinegar

# Friendly Faces, Friendly Places

## Some Friends and Places
## in This Book

Name the stories you liked best.
Read them to your friends so they will know
them, too.

230

231

## Word List

Included in this list are all words used in Inside and Out which have not appeared in earlier levels of PATHFINDER —Allyn and Bacon Reading Program.

The words are listed in the order of their introduction in each story. The number at the left indicates the page on which a word first appears.

The words are classified into three types:

**Foundation Words:** Words which will appear repeatedly in the program. These are the foundation of the children's reading vocabulary and are given special emphasis in instruction.

**Skill-based Words:** Words which most children should be able to read independently by applying decoding skills taught either in earlier lessons at this level or at previous levels. Skill-based words in this list are printed in **boldface** type.

**Story-specific Words:** Words which are important to the understanding of a particular selection but which are not systematically maintained or reused at this level. Many of these words will recur in pupils' recreational reading and most will be in the listening and speaking vocabularies of most of the children. Story-specific words in this list are printed in *italics.*

Variant forms of previously introduced words are not considered new to the program if the generalization for forming the variant has been taught. Also not considered new are compounds formed from known parts, contractions formed from known parts using previously learned generalizations, and words which are parts of previously learned compounds.

6. *Martha*
**pea**
**pots**
*George*
hated
anything
**tell**
8. himself
**drop**
9. *kitchen*
rest
*shoes*
10. **feel**
11. *silly*
12. *cookies*
13. *Katy*
*Father*
14. most
*alone*
walks
**sand**
sailing
**herself**
15. *summer*
*gull*
talked
again
17. *I'd*
**maybe**
ask
19. **forget**
*sadly*
20. *winter*

hope
he's
21. *spring*
let's
22. **nest**
23. *Samantha*
24. *Judy*
*Jody*
*twins*
or
*teacher*
25. *Aunt*
25. **Bee**
stay
few
**everything**
**same**
28. **that's**
*different*
29. **bed**
30. low
31. should
32. **rope**
*learned*
picture
33. **today**
34. **way**
35. *morning*
36. *Mei Ling*
*apartment*
two
**Pam**
*upstairs*

*Nancy*
*downstairs*
*middle*
37. read
*dumb*
40. **bin**
*kitten*
**into**
**deep**
cry
41. hold
*while*
**I'll**
try
43. *reached*
44. together
*O.K.*
52. **Bim**
*Bim-Bam*
53. **tall**
*Terry*
*tomorrow*
55. *studio*
**drove**
56. once
*stopped*
**late**
57. *elephant*
*Emma*
*follow*
60. **isn't**
*biggest*
61. *sign*

62. *Sarah*
**Jack**
climb
*apples*
*Horrible Hank*
**kids**
**called**
**pest**
**who's**
65. *ladder*
66. **you'll**
**Tip**
**wasn't**
noise
68. **plan**
71. **Pine**
**town**
72. *streets*
stores
words
**pictures**
73. *mayor*
75. glasses
find
76. **wish**
77. soon
**mixed**
81. **places**
86. *happened*
*Susan*
**Miles**
**yet**
*garage*

**tow truck**
friendly
87. cars
**flat**
**tires**
88. *hello*
**plane**
**freeway**
police
90. our
92. everyone
100. **pit**
cried
**can't**
101. **top**
102. tried
**broke**
use
104. *coconut*
*roll*
*angry*
*stomped*
**upset**
106. **didn't**
small
115. *roared*
tired
116. *Bee bee bobbi bobbi*
baby
please
117. **wide**
*awake*
**aren't**

long
118. **dear**
119. keeper
*asleep*
120. quietly
123. *moved*
even
127. **cooking**
129. *Skohottentot*
been
131. *Skolinkenlot*
133. birds
134. seven
girls
*dancing*
136. **pink**
*parasol*
139. **cut**
144. kinds
somebody
children
145. neighbors
149. *Simon Rodia*
*Los Angeles*
*towers*
151. *junk*
*bottles*
**cups**
spoons
**nails**
**pipe**
152. *wonderful*
*castle*

153. **near**
154. **safe**
156. *Watts*
160. **painter**
    **everybody**
    sister
    brother
    *Alberto*
    boat
161. *idea*
162. pretty
163. **faces**
    *Alex Lazaro*
164. **policeman**
166. **belong**
    **such**
167. **wait**
169. *Tony*
170. **pay**
    their
    **helpers**
171. **hug**
172. *mountain*
173. **hardly**
    flowers
    **gray**
    **nobody**
    *ever*
174. **Rap**
    **free**
175. Ms.
    *Plunkett*
    love

177. stories
178. **train**
179. better
180. *secret*
181. *magic*
193. *salad*
    *Max*
    **dig**
    **rake**
    *Carla*
    *Uncle*
    **Jay**
    making
    *vegetable*
194. **we'll**
    family
    **weed**
196. **fresh**
198. **sun**
200. **mess**
201. *Mama*
202. **Sunday**
    coming
    *dinner*
206. **ant**
209. *leaves*
    ground
210. **queen**
    **lay**
    **workers**
211. *rooms*
212. food
    chew

    **parts**
213. *juices*
    larger
    **itself**
    *strong*
214. **another**
    **rub**
    *bodies*
    **hear**
    *these*
    sounds
217. *account*
    *dinosaur*
    **cave**
    **sticking**
218. flew
    **overhead**
221. *class*
222. *lunch*
    *Dandy*
    *Tutt*
223. *paper*
    **seemed**
    **shake**
224. *Doctor Bright*
    *wondered*
225. gym
226. *shaking*
    *you're*
    *loud*
228. *mind*
    *scientist*

*Acknowledgments (continued from page ii)*

"The Baby Beebee Bird," adapted from *The Baby Beebee Bird* by Diane Redfield Massie. Copyright © 1963 by Diane Redfield Massie. Reprinted by permission of Harper & Row, Publishers, Inc.

"Riddles," from *Hey Riddle Diddle* by Rodney Peppe. Copyright © 1971 by Rodney Peppe. Reprinted by permission of Holt, Rinehart and Winston, Publishers.

"The Fat Cat," from *The Fat Cat* translated and illustrated by Jack Kent. Copyright © 1971 by Jack Kent. By permission of Parents' Magazine Press.

"Castle in My City," © 1968 Patty Zeitlin.

"Weather Is Full of the Nicest Sounds," copyright © 1963 by Aileen Fisher from *I Like Weather* by Aileen Fisher with permission of Thomas Y. Crowell Company, Inc.

"Who Has Seen the Wind," from *Sing-Song* by Christina G. Rossetti. Copyright 1924 by the Macmillan Publishing Co., Inc. All rights reserved.

"Take a Look at Ants," text copyright © 1975, by Gray Johnson Poole. Used by permission.

"Ants Live Here," text copyright © 1967 by Lilian Moore. From *I Feel the Same Way.* Used by permission of Atheneum Publishers.

"Quiet on Account of Dinosaur," by Jane Thayer. Adapted by permission of William Morrow & Company, Inc. Copyright © 1964 by Catherine Wooley.

Selections in this book not otherwise credited are by Mark Taylor.

**Illustrations:** Leigh Grant p. 1; Marc Brown pp. 2-5; James Marshall pp. 7-9, 11, 12; Hal Frenck pp. 13-23; John Wallner pp. 24-35; Heidi Palmer pp. 36-45; Susan Banta pp. 46-48; Leigh Grant p. 49; Ethel Gold pp. 50-51; Creston Ely pp. 52-61; Monica Santa pp. 63-65, 67-70; David McPhail pp. 71-81; Kees de Kiefte pp. 82-85; Joel Snyder pp. 86, 87, 89-93; Amy Myers pp. 94-95; Susan Banta pp. 96-98; Leigh Grant p. 99; Bill Morrison pp. 100-103, 105, 106; Andrea Da Rif pp. 107-114; Carol Nicklaus pp. 115-123; Jared Lee pp. 124-126; Jack Kent pp. 127-133, 135-139; Susan Banta pp. 140-142; Leigh Grant p. 143; Rudolph Robinson p. 144 right and bottom right; Betsy Cole p. 144 middle left; Rudolph Robinson p. 145 top left; Betsy Cole p. 145 top right; Owen Franken, Stock, Boston p. 145 bottom; Diane Lowe p. 146 bottom; Fredrik D. Bodin p. 146 top right and middle right; Steve Dunwell photo p. 146 top left; Steve Dunwell photo p. 147 top left; John Running p. 147 top right; Fritz Bernstein p. 147 bottom right; Diane Lowe p. 147 bottom left; Steven M. Stone p. 148 bottom right; Rudolph Robinson p. 148 middle left; John Running p. 148 top left; Fritz Bernstein p. 148 middle right; Yoram Kahana from Peter Arnold p. 149; George Hall from Woodfin Camp p. 150 top left; Yoram Kahana from Peter Arnold p. 150 bottom left; Peter Arnold p. 150 right; Yoram Kahana from Peter Arnold p. 151, 152; Vic Cox from Peter Arnold p. 153; Yoram Kahana from Peter Arnold p. 154; Vic Cox from Peter Arnold p. 155, 156 right; Yoram Kahana from Peter Arnold p. 156 left; Amy Myers pp. 157-159; Phil Smith pp. 160-171; Ikki Matsumoto pp. 172-181; Annie Gusman pp. 182-185; Susan Banta pp. 186-188; Leigh Grant p. 189; Ikki Matsumoto pp. 190-192; Janet Palmer pp. 193-204; Stella Ormai p. 205; Jan Wills pp. 206-215; Bill Davis p. 216; Rick Brown pp. 217-225, 227, 228; Susan Banta pp. 229-231.

All photographs not otherwise credited are the work of the Allyn and Bacon staff photographers.

236